KV-061-047

In Touch

Internet and E-mail

Angela Royston

www.heinemann.co.uk/library
Visit our website to find out more information about **Heinemann Library** books.

To order:
☎ Phone ++44 (0)1865 888066
▤ Send a fax to ++44 (0)1865 314091
▢ Visit the Heinemann Bookshop at www.heinemann.co.uk/library to browse our
catalogue and order online.

First published in Great Britain by Heinemann Library, Halley Court, Jordan Hill, Oxford
OX2 8EJ, a division of Reed Educational and Professional Publishing Ltd. Heinemann
is a registered trademark of Reed Educational & Professional Publishing Ltd.

OXFORD MELBOURNE AUCKLAND JOHANNESBURG BLANTYRE
GABORONE IBADAN PORTSMOUTH NH (USA) CHICAGO

© Reed Educational and Professional Publishing Ltd 2001
The moral right of the proprietor has been asserted.

All rights reserved. No part of this publication may be reproduced, stored in a retrieval system,
or transmitted in any form or by any means, electronic, mechanical, photocopying, recording,
or otherwise without either the prior written permission of the Publishers or a licence
permitting restricted copying in the United Kingdom issued by the Copyright Licensing
Agency Ltd, 90 Tottenham Court Road, London W1P 0LP.

Designed by Visual Image
Illustrations by Visual Image
Originated by Ambassador Litho Ltd.
Printed in Hong Kong/China

05 04 03 02 01
10 9 8 7 6 5 4 3 2 1

ISBN 0431 11285 1

British Library Cataloguing in Publication Data

Royston, Angela
  Internet and e-mail. – (In touch)
  1. Internet – Juvenile literature
  2. Electronic mail systems – Juvenile literature
  I. Title
  004.6'78

Acknowledgements

The Publishers would like to thank the following for permission to reproduce photographs:
Associated Press Photos: p10; Bob Battersby: p13; Borders: p24; Bush Internet: p11; Corbis: pp6,
28, Commander John Leenhouts p29; Earthlink: p8; Google: p21; Microsoft: pp14, 16, 17; NASA:
p20; R.D. Battersby: p12; San Diego Zoo: p22; Sega: p26; Stockbyte: p23; Stone: p4, Hunter
Freeman p18, Walter Hodges p5, Steven Peters p27; The Stock Market: p15; Trevor Clifford: p9;
WWF: p19.

Cover photograph reproduced with permission of Trevor Clifford.

Every effort has been made to contact copyright holders of any material reproduced in this book.
Any omissions will be rectified in subsequent printings if notice is given to the Publisher.

Contents

Any words appearing in the text in bold, **like this**, are explained in the Glossary.

Communications

Communications are different ways of talking to people. Television, radio, post, telephone, newspapers and the Internet are all types of communication.

The Internet

This book tells you what the Internet is. It also explains how the Internet works and how people use it.

Children use computers to help them learn and to find out information. These children are looking at the Internet on their computer.

Internet uses

You may have used the Internet yourself. The Internet lets you find out information from other computers. It also lets people talk to each other and send messages called **e-mails** from one computer to another.

Telephone link

You can only use the Internet if you have a computer linked to a telephone. The telephone connects your computer to millions of other computers.

Many people have a computer at home. They use e-mail to keep in touch with their friends and family.

Linking computers

Computers that are linked together are called a **network**. The Internet is a huge network that stretches around the world.

All the computers that are connected to the Internet can send messages to each other.

Simple networks

Sometimes all the computers in one office are linked to a main computer. This computer is called a **server**. It holds the information stored in all the other office computers.

Everyone in this office has their own computer. All the computers are linked together to form a network. This means that people can send e-mail messages to each other on their computers.

Internet servers

The Internet is too big to have one main computer. So it has several servers that are connected to each other. These are called **Internet servers**. You have to join one of these, called an **Internet Service Provider (ISP)**, to use the Internet.

The Internet network

Internet servers are linked together by special telephone lines and **satellites**. Together they form one huge network.

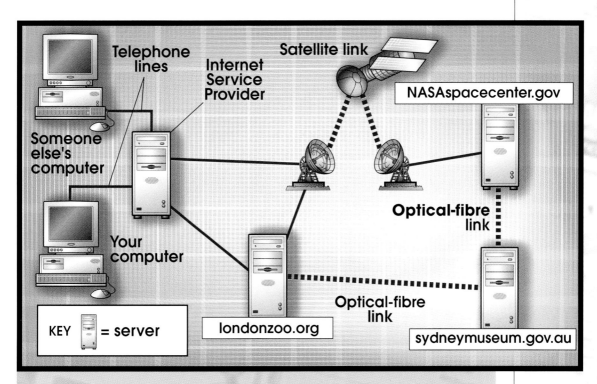

Each computer is linked to an Internet server. There are hundreds of servers. Each one is linked to all the others. This makes a huge network of linked computers.

Logging on

Logging on means getting connected to the Internet. To do this you must belong to one of the **Internet Service Providers**. This is what happens when you log on.

Going on-line

Your computer can telephone your Internet Service Provider, using an ordinary telephone line. Once your computer is linked to the **server**, you are then '**on-line**'.

This Internet Service Provider is called EarthLink. There are hundreds of different ISPs to choose from.

Using the Net

Once you are on-line you can use the Internet in several ways. You can send an **e-mail** or you can look up information held on other computers. You can even buy things over the Internet.

A special box called a modem links your computer to the telephone. New computers have a modem inside them.

Going off-line

When you have finished using the Internet, you break off the telephone link with your server. Your computer is then '**off-line**'.

Fast and cheap

Sending an e-mail is much cheaper than telephoning. You write the message first and then log on for a few seconds to send it.

TVs and phones

You can also use some telephones and televisions to link up with the Internet.

Internet phones

Some telephones have their own computer with a small screen. The computer lets you send **e-mails** or find information on the Internet.

Some computers are so small you can hold them in one hand! You can use this palm-top computer to log on to the Internet.

Televisions

You can also **log on** to the Internet with a **digital** television. Some **games consoles** can log on too.

One machine for everything

In the past, people had a machine for each form of **communication**. Soon you will be able to get one machine that does everything. You will use it to rent films by telephone, to log on to the Internet and to watch television.

At one time you had to own an expensive computer to get on to the Internet. Now you can log on from some televisions and phones.

E-mails

Sending an **e-mail** is like posting a letter but much quicker. The other person can receive it a few seconds later, even if they are on the other side of the world.

Postbox for e-mails

Your **Internet Service Provider** acts as a postbox. It sends and receives your e-mails for you. You receive the e-mails when you log on to your **server**.

Sending an e-mail is as fast as making a phone call. The computer screen shows the e-mails you send and those you receive.

You can use this telephone to send and receive e-mail messages. You press the number buttons to key in the letters of each word.

E-mail address

Your postal address tells the post office exactly where you live. In the same way, people who use e-mail have their own e-mail address. It gives your e-mail name and the name of your ISP.

Writing an e-mail address

An e-mail address is written on one line, like this:
e-mailname@ISP.com
You have to write the e-mail address exactly right. If you miss out anything, the computer will not recognize it.

Sending an e-mail

To write a new **e-mail**, click on your computer screen where it says 'New mail message'. Then enter the e-mail address of the person you are sending the message to.

Replying to an e-mail

You can also reply to a message you have received by clicking on 'Reply'. The computer then writes the e-mail address for you. All you have to do then is type your message above the old message.

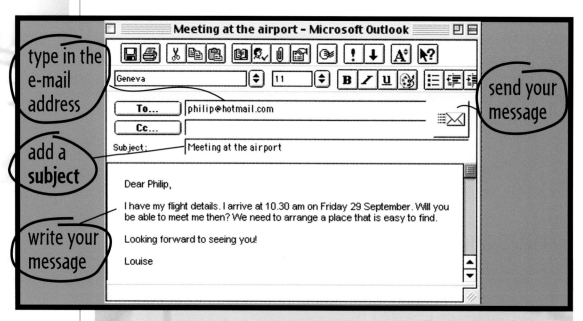

This computer screen shows you how to write and send an e-mail message. You need to know the e-mail address of the person you are writing to.

Sending the message

When you have written your message, click on 'Send'. If you are already **on-line**, the computer sends the e-mail straight away.

If you are **off-line**, the computer dials the **Internet Service Provider** to connect you. You can see on your screen when the e-mail is sent.

If you do not have a computer at home, you can go to a library. Here you can use a computer to go on the Internet and send e-mails.

Getting an e-mail

When someone sends you an **e-mail** it does not come straight to your computer. It is stored on a **server** at your **Internet Service Provider**. You can check from time to time to see if you have any new messages.

Getting new messages

When you click on 'Get new mail', your computer sends your special **password** to your server. The server checks your mailbox and sends any messages to your computer.

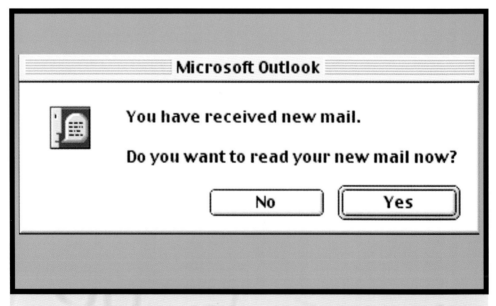

People in offices are usually connected to their server all the time. The computer checks for e-mails and displays the message shown here.

16

Attachments

E-mails sometimes have other **documents** attached to them. The **attachment** can be a drawing, a photo, or a document stored somewhere else in the computer.

Copying messages

You can send the same message to more than one person. The computer copies the message to each address you type in.

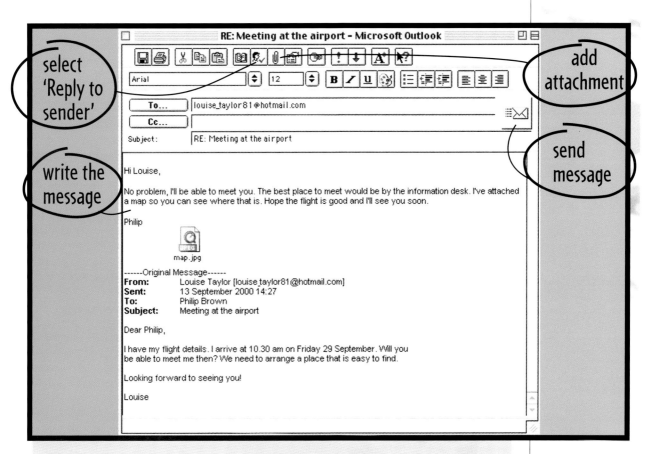

This computer screen shows how to reply to a message and add an attachment. The attachment travels with the e-mail as a separate document.

The World Wide Web

You can use the Internet to find out information. The **World Wide Web (Web)** is the name we use for all the pages of information stored on the Internet. It is like a huge library that you can look at without leaving your home.

What's on the Web?

The Web is made up of millions of **websites**. Each site gives information about something in particular, for example a football team, dinosaurs, or space. New sites are added to the Web every day.

People everywhere use computers. They can look up information held on **servers** all around the world.

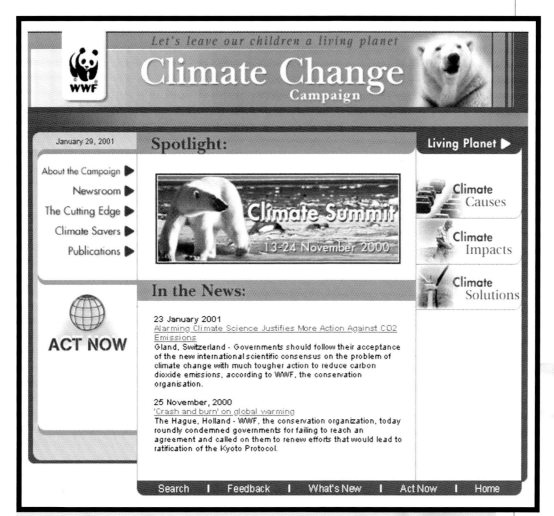

This is part of the website of a conservation organization.
This page tells you about the organization's activities.

Web pages

A website often has several **web pages**.
These are like the pages of a book.
They may have pictures as well as words.
They may have sounds and short pieces
of video too.

You can move from one page to another
by clicking on special links. These might
be words or pictures.

Surfing the Web

Looking at **websites** is sometimes called surfing the **Web**.

Web browser

A **web browser** is a special computer **program** that helps you find a website. It also **downloads** the **web pages**. This means it copies the pages on to your computer.

A browser lets you choose a website and copy it on to your computer. This website gives information about space.

This is the website of the search engine called Google. You have to type in the subject that you want it to search for. It then shows you the best ten sites that it finds.

Search engines

A **search engine** is a special website that searches through the Web for a particular **subject** that you want.

A search engine knows the addresses of millions of websites and what is stored on their pages. It can check through millions of websites for a particular subject in just a few seconds.

Exploring a website

Every **website** has a website address. A website address is like an **e-mail** address, except that it always begins 'www'.

Where is the website?

A website is really just a collection of computer files stored on a **server**. When you enter the address of a website into your **web browser**, the browser finds the server where the website is stored.

This website shows moving video pictures of a panda's life. Pictures and music take longer to download than words. Moving pictures take the longest of all.

Downloading

The server sends the files that make up the website back to your computer. The computer files are then **downloaded** and shown on your screen.

Passwords

Most websites can be read by anybody. But some sites are protected by a **password**. Only people who have the password can read the information.

This phone is a WAP telephone. It can download web pages from the Internet. Phones like this are becoming cheaper to buy.

Building a website

You can build a **website** using a special computer **program**. Large companies pay experts to make a website for them. Web designers work out the pages.

Buying on the Internet

A website tells you about a company. Many websites let you buy things. Only adults who have credit cards can buy on the Internet.

Many companies build their own websites. This is a page from the website of a company that sells books. The list on the left shows the areas included in the website.

This is a **digital** camera. It takes pictures that can be put easily on to a computer and used to build a website.

Building a website

You need many people to build a big website. First someone must decide what information the website should give. Next, designers divide the information into pages and make links between them.

The pages are sent to an **Internet server** which sends the website address to several **search engines**. Now everyone can find the site on the Internet!

Internet groups

A newsgroup is a group of people who use the Internet to discuss a particular **subject**. There are thousands of different newsgroups. If you have an unusual pet, you will probably find a newsgroup on it.

Notice-board

A newsgroup is like a notice-board. You can read messages from other people in the group. You can also send messages for other people to read.

Many people like to play with **games consoles** like this one. Some link their computers through the Internet and play against each other.

These people are having a business meeting. They each have a camera and microphone attached to their computers so they can see and hear each other.

Chat rooms

A chat room allows people to speak to each other by typing messages on to their computers. Everyone who is connected to the chat room sees the message on their screen.

You must be very careful if you join a chat room. Never give your real name or address. Use a pretend name, such as 'Big Cat'. Ask your parent or teacher before you use a chat room.

Internet times

Here are some important events in the history of the Internet.

1940s The first computers are used. They are so big they fill whole rooms.

1947 Special switches called **transistors** are invented.

1959 Silicon chips are invented. Along with transistors, they make computers faster and smaller.

1969 Computers in different places are linked together in a **network**. The computers belong to a group working for the United States' armed forces.

Telstar was the first communications satellite. It was launched into space in 1962. Satellites made the Internet possible.

This building is called the Pentagon. It is the headquarters of the United States' armed forces. It was here that the Internet began.

1970s The first **e-mail** is sent in the Pentagon, in the USA.

1980s Networks in many countries are linked to make a worldwide network.

1989 The **World Wide Web** is set up. **Web browsers** begin soon after.

1990s Internet Service Providers begin. Now ordinary people can use the Internet too.

2001 Many mobile phones and televisions can **log on** to the Internet.

Glossary

attachment something that is added on

communication way of sending and receiving information

digital something that uses signals that are read by computers

document piece of paper or computer file which contains information

download copy from one computer to another

e-mail written message sent from one computer to another

games console simple computer used only for playing computer games

Internet server very powerful computer that stores information on the Internet

Internet Service Provider (ISP) company that connects your computer to the Internet

log on connect your computer to the Internet

network two or more computers linked together

off-line not connected to an Internet Service Provider

on-line connected to an Internet Service Provider

optical fibre cable which carries messages as light signals

password secret word that only chosen people know

program set of instructions that tell a computer what to do

satellite object in space that circles round the Earth

search engine website that searches through the World Wide Web to look for particular subjects

server powerful computer which stores information for all computers linked to it

silicon chip very small electrical circuit

subject topic

transistor a kind of switch

web browser computer program that allows you to look at the World Wide Web

web page information from a website shown on the screen at one time

website collection of information about a particular subject stored on the Internet

World Wide Web (Web) huge collection of information stored in websites on the Internet

Index

Titles in the *In Touch* series:

Hardback   0 431 11285 1

Hardback   0 431 11280 0

Hardback   0 431 11284 3

Hardback   0 431 11281 9

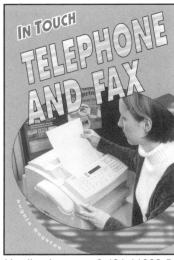

Hardback   0 431 11283 5

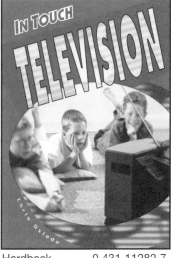

Hardback   0 431 11282 7

Find out about other Heinemann resources on our website www.heinemann.co.uk/library